To: God Gloria

Sister I thank you so very much.

Love

Danny Glover

Wings of the Whirlwind

Published by
Queen's Palace Productions
P.O. Box 571
Bladensburg, MD 20710
(301) 927-0670

Wings Of The Whirlwind

(Tribute to the Honorable Marcus M. Garvey)

Look for me
I'm coming back again
No matter, where I am
Or just where I've been
In the eye of the storm
You'll see me again
In the spirit of the new birth
On the wings of the whirlwind

Wings of the Whirlwind

Poems by

Daniel R. Queen

Copyright©1989 by Daniel R. Queen

All rights reserved. No part of this book may be reproduced or transmitted in any form by any means, electronic or mechanical, including photocopying and recording, or by any information storage or retrieval system, without permission in writing from the publisher

ISBN-1-881328-00-7

Dedication/Acknowledgements

First, I would like to thank God for His gift of life; my mother Frances L. Queen; my sisters, Gloria, Mary Jane, Rose, Anita, Zina, and Wanda; and my brothers, James and Robert, for their love and support.

I give much thanks to my mentor of many years, Dr. Dorothy S. Smith of Bowie State University; Dr. Virginia B. Guilford of the Department of Humanities and Fine Arts, Bowie State University; John Raye and Mrs. Rose Smith; Phil Mastuizo, of the *Prince Georges Journal*, for the back cover photograph.

I also thank the Rev. Willie Wilson of Union Temple Baptist Church, Washington, D.C.; Dr. Abdul Alim Muhammad. Captain William Muhammad, FOI, Brother Abdul Wali Muhammad, editor of *The Final Call* newspaper; Barry Murray, editor of the Capital Spot Light, Washington, D.C.; Brother Hodari Addual Ali of Pyramid Books; Proteen Mabry for the cover design and illustration; FOI Mosque No. 4; Sister Cathy Hughes, WMMJ/WOL 1450 AM, Washington, D.C.; and Deborah Squirewell.

Write to:
Wings of the Whirlwind
Danny R. Queen
P.O. Box 571
Bladensburg, Maryland 20710
Phone (301) 927-0670

Foreword

It was the great liberator, Marcus Garvey, who thundered nearly 50 years ago, "Up you mighty race..., you can do what you will!" Garvey was a visionary who mounted the greatest movement of black people ever in this country. Unlike any other black leader, Garvey organized black people. No other black leader, before or since, has ever matched or duplicated his amazing feats.

In a very short time span, he literally transformed a downtrodden and backward people into a giant of immense power and social responsibility. Garvey was more than a man in human form, he was spirit; an invisible man who came and left us in the middle of a whirlwind. Though the United States government broke his movement, deported him to England and forced him to waste away in prison, Garvey's spirit was never broken.

Poet/Writer Daniel Queen, in this penetrating and mind-expanding volume, *Wings of the Whirlwind*, has recaptured the spirit and the essence of Garvey. The volume is a powerful and vivid reminder of the great Garvey spirit that has returned to liberate black people the world over.

Garvey never did die because he told his enemies that he would "return in the whirlwind." We must know that spirit never dies, it is only transformed. Queen, a powerful writer, reflects the great wisdom and insight of Garvey. Not only will you read Garvey's message in Queen's stimulating poems, but you will feel, yes, actually experience the Garvey spirit.

Garvey reminds us to focus and to stay the course. His pace was so stupendous that it is unlikely to ever be matched, probably not in our lifetime. Queen has provided us with a very powerful weapon, and that weapon is information. Garvey was about information. Since we now live in the Information Age, control and power will remain in the hands of those who control information.

Garvey knew all alone that information was power. His organizational skills and his immense power came from his ability to control and organize information about the Garvey spirit. Indeed, it is no accident, that so little information is available about Garvey today. It is all by design, a calculated effort to discredit and dismiss one of the greatest human liberators to ever walk this earth.

In *Wings of the Whirlwind*, Garvey lives again. It is the jarring prose of Queen's tenacious spirit that reconnects both the messenger and the message. Just as he said he would, Garvey is back to haunt us and to remind us of our mission and purpose. It was spirit that brought us over here, and it was spirit that enable us to survive and prosper in a land that never welcomed nor invited us.

Garvey's spirit is alive and well again. Go now, please, in the following pages, and greet your brother in the whirlwind.

John Raye,
President of the Majestic Eagles,
Washington, DC.
September, 1989.

Introduction

Daniel Queen is a young man, who earlier in his life resolved to become a poet of the people. In preparing for this missionary role, he began to devour the African-American literary legacy and later the whole of African-American culture, becoming awed by its heroes and sensitive to the paradoxical beauty and pain of his long line of ancestors.

Daniel's own literary career, in a sense, embodies the spirit of his ancestors. He has defied statistics which clearly say that he should not be by his own tenacious perseverance, ingenuity and humanity. Yes, Daniel was nurtured by an establish disbelievers, but he remained undaunted, and now his courted audience is beginning to speak, to embrace this young poet who defied the odds to preserve the soul of the contemporary African-American. The masses, young African-American college students and those who seek not food for the mind, but for the soul, are testifying to Daniel Queen's own self-proclamation:

> *I am the Life of a People's*
> *Long Lost Sense of Pride*
> *I am the Hopes and Dreams*
> *Locked Away Deep Down Inside.*

In this, his first collection of works, stimulated by the spirit of Marcus Garvey, poet and lyricist Daniel Queen continues to speak to the people.

Virginia B. Guilford,
Department of Humanities and Fine Arts,
Bowie State University

Tributes

The poetry of Danny Queen is truly a reflection of the black experience. It's a unique, multi-faceted gift to express human emotion. It is rough, exciting, stimulating and must be read to be heard. Its ability surpasses contemporary literature and with the quality of his truth, he reminds us that to avoid repeating mistakes in the future, we must ever be mindful of the past. Danny Queen is obviously not afraid to be black.

> Larry Bland,
> President of the American
> Congress
> for Economic Reform

Brother Danny Queen, through poetic expression, has been able to present a truthful mosaic of African-American characters and experiences in America. His work covers the full spectrum of the African-American experience—its culture, its problems, and its ever-present sense of overcoming spirituality.

It took the preacher/prophet Paul to analyze the past, evaluate the present and prognosticate about the future. I very much identify with Danny's insightful analysis of the African-American mind, spirit and soul. I am more than sure that all who read this work will appreciate his talent and ability.

> The Rev. Willie F. Wilson,
> Union Temple Baptist Church,
> Washington, D.C., 1989

Brother Danny is a vibrant and creative voice of our people. He finds beauty among our people. His words are lyrical and are music to the ears. Most importantly, he has something significant to say—that there is hope, love and progress in the history the present and the future of our people.

> Hodari Addul (Ali),
> Proprietor of Pyramid Bookstore,
> Washington, D.C.

Contents

The Non-Violent Warrior	1
Danny's Love	2
Walkie-Talkie (Part I)	2
The Junk Food Blues (Part I)	3
The Junk Food Blues (Part 2)	4
Angel Dust Heaven	4
Priceless	5
The Lyrics of a Song	6
Not the Marrying Kind (Part I)	7
Windows of My Mind	7
Lady-Lovesmith	8
The Sweetheart Swindler	8
Like a Movin' Target	9
First Impressions	10
Love Me, For Me	10
Miss Bad Little Honey	11
Let God Be God	12
First Things First	13
Love Finds Its Own Way	13
Then Came You	14
Inflation	15
His Story (Part I)	16
His Story (Part II)	16
Unless We Learn to Love	17
Act No. 1	18
Act No. 2	18
Private Lines	18
Toys 'R' Us	19
All Rights Reserved (Part I)	20
All Rights Reserved (Part II)	21
Chocolate City Candy	21
The Grace of Faith	22
South Africa: The Cesspool	23
Apartheid	24
Jesus Paid the Cost	25
Pain	25
Time	26
'Natural High'	26
When You Give of Yourself	26

On the Wings of Success	27
Self-Service	27
Thankful Thinkin'	28
With Eyes of A Child	28
Sound Experience	28
Everybody Has A Dream	28
Family	29
The Only Heaven I Know	29
Marriage Can Be A Monster	29
1600 Pennsylvania Avenue	30
Blue-Eyed Booty	31
No Cream in the Coffee	32
Blue-Black Honey	33
Every Day Is Mother's Day	33
Some Christians	34
The Father's Day Poem	35
Information Is Power	35
A Raye of Hope	37
The Dark Side of A Star	37
_____'s Love	38
How Do I Say 'Thank You'?	39
Only Always	40
A Poet of the People	40
Don't Add Loss to Loss	41
Pride and Joy	43
The Moody Booty Blues	44
A Prayer	44
Forever Somebody	45
A Message to Michael	45
Let's Make A Baby	47
Long Live the Memory	48
It Ain't What Ya Know	48
What Color Was Jesus?	49
Times: 19 and 29	50
Love Don't Live By Sex Alone	51
Everybody's Out Ta Lunch	52
I Am Because God Is	53
Hotline to Heaven	53
Deep And Quiet Love	54
Soul in the Super Bowl	55
Everybody's Somebody's Fool	56
The Epic Hero	58

The Graduation Poem	59
Say NO to Drugs	59
Babies Making Babies	60
Endangered Species	61
From A Friend to A Friend	63
From No-Hope to New-Hope	64
Where Will My People Be?	65
Ebony Lady	66
Love's False Fire	66
Life ain't about nothin'	67
Scared Straight	68
Keep on Smiling	69
Pen Man	69
POWER	69
Black Family	70
I Could Never Love Another	71
Food for Thought	71
A World Without Love	71
The Imperial Night	72
First Class Friendship	73
The Ugly People Poem	74
Black and Blue	74
Search for Tomorrow	75
Love Somebody	76
Bleeding Black Hearts	76
Still A Star In My Heart	77
Let's Talk about It	77
20th Century Fox	78
Walkie-Talkie (Part II)	79
Color Me Poetry	79
White Supremacy	81
Quin-essence	83
The Godfather of Soul	84
The Most Divine One	85
Conscience Control	86

The Non-Violent Warrior
(For Rev. Dr. Martin Luther King, Jr.)

When we keep the legacies
Of Love and Truth alive,
All life's timeless hopes
And dreams will survive.

Oh, they killed the dreamer,
But the dream still lives on
Of a non-violent soldier who
Tried to right what was wrong.

He was a non-violent warrior
On the battlefield of injustice,
As living proof that his words of wisdom
Were his only weapon of truth.

He was a prophet for peace.
A spiritual keynote from above,
He was a drum major for justice
And a locksmith for love.

Oh, they killed the dreamer,
But the dream still lives on
Of a non-violent soldier who
Tried to right what was wrong.

He tried to unlock the vaults
Of oppression for the family of man
When he put his fate's destiny
In the Master's hand.

Thus the melody of brotherhood
Through all struggle and strife
Will someday find perfect harmony
On the keyboard of life.

Danny's Love

Someway, someday, somehow,
I'll be your blessing in disguise.
Like a genie from outta nowhere,
I'll appear right before your very eyes.

Becuz my love for you is so deep
That it cuts like a knife
Through all pain, misery, and strife,
Just to give to you the gift of
My love for life.

Now I may not be a world-famed
Shining super star, or ride in
A custom made fancy car, but the
Likes of my love for you is so
Much better by far.

And though I don't have money
Or expensive gifts to give out
At will, when you trust in the
Treasures of Danny's love, you
Gonna know just how I feel.

Becuz my love for you is so deep
That it cuts like a knife
Through all the pain, misery, and strife,
Just to give to you the gift of
My love for life...Danny's love.

Walkie-Talkie
(Part I)

Always tunin' in and turnin' on
Tryin' to catch a line, you're just a
Walkie-Talkie, walkin' 'n' talkin'
All the time.

Tunin' in and turnin' on
Singin' the same old song, 'bout he say she say.

Startin' a ball of confusion, dragin' a chain
Of lies; you bring the news with a new surprise.

You're always out in the street
Lyin' 'n' signifyin' smokin' 'n' jokin'
Walkin' 'n' talkin' from house to house
To lend an ear to all you can find out.

You spend umteem hours on the telephone
Mindin' everybody's business but your own.
For only the gossip of hearsay can make you
Feel at home.

The Junk Food Blues
(Part 1)

If you're on the run
Or just out havin' fun,
Don't stuff yourself like a hog
With death burgers and hot dogs.

When you start to feel like
You're only half alive, then
You'll realize you don't need
All that junk food jive to stay alive.

Fresh fruit 'n' natural foods
Will do your body more than a
Great deal of good, if you take
The time to eat like you should.

And unless you've got a stomach
Made of steel, ain't nothin' like
The real deal, which is a full
Course home-cooked meal.

The Junk Food Blues
(Part 2)

Some things you eat
Would turn your stomach inside out
If you really knew what you
Were puttin' in your mouth.

'Cause it takes more than
Cookies and cakes
And chocolate milkshakes
To make you feel like you've
Had some kinda meal.

For the non-protein fast foods
Of Burger King, Hardees, Wendy's,
And Mickey D's are bad enough
To bring a bionic elephant to
His knees.

So if you deserve a break today,
And you must have it your way, please,
Don't have no Big Mac attack
When all you need is a tasty break
With a balanced snack....

Angel Dust Heaven

Caught up in the outer limits
Of the twilight zone;
Lost between reality 'n' dream
In a world of your own.

There you stand
With a heart full of headaches
In the palm of your hand. Check out
Your mind and give yourself a chance.

An angel dust heaven
Is a hopeless high that only pacifies.
Angel dust heaven is a hopeless high.

There ain't a drug that's not a drag
When walkin' in your sleep up a no-return
Street, hope just turns to dope.

Helplessly hooked on a hopeless high,
You slipped into the future and fought
With your fate, found your head,
But couldn't put it on straight.

An angel dust heaven
Is a hopeless high that only pacifies.
Angel dust heaven is a hopeless high.

Pleasure is pain
And heaven becomes hell
When that hopeless high has
Intensified and left you full of emptiness inside.

An angel dust heaven
Is a hopeless high.

Priceless

When nothin' beats a failure
But a try, you're that special kinda
Guy, who never fails to freely give
The things that money can't buy.

Diamonds, emeralds and pearls
Can't begin to compare
To all the love in our hearts
That we share.

Preciously priceless
That's what you are to me.
Preciously priceless as any love
Could ever be. Preciously priceless.

You've been better to me
Than I've been to myself.
You're my pearl of pure
Pleasure and all of my wealth.

When it comes to lovin' me,
You're a millionaire without
A dime to your name; you're my
One and only claim to fortune
And fame, and to my heart's delight.
At last the price is right.

Preciously priceless.
That's what you are to me.
Preciously priceless as any love
Could ever be.
Preciously priceless.

The Lyrics of a Song

Think of me as a broken record
If you will, but in an instant
Replay I'll say the same thing
Still, 'cause when it comes to
Having a moral message in the
Music, this is truly how I feel.

If the lyrics of a song
Can't give you strength enough
To be strong, then it's not worth
The groove it's recorded on.

Don't be fooled by the amenity
Of mindless, messageless words
And music; when you know in your
Heart that your soul can't use it.

When there's no message
Or glory in the story of a song,
What good is the rhythm or rhyme
Without words of wisdom for all mankind?

'Cause if the lyrics of a song
Can't give you strength enough
To be strong, then it's not worth
The groove it's recorded on.

Not the Marrying Kind
(Part I)

If and when
I ever decide to tie
The knot of love and romance,
Let it be by choice and not by chance.

When push comes to shove
And like turns to love,
I may surely meet my match,
But until then there'll be no strings attached.

For better or for worse
The promise of love, may or may not
Keep love afloat, when the tidal waves
Of hard times suddenly rocks the boat.

A seemingly true love at first sight
Might catch some guys' eye, but I've
Seen and heard it all before, and I
Don't want to live another lie.

So I've finally made up my mind
That I am not the marrying kind.

Windows of My Mind

Through the windows of my mind
And the darkness that I find,
There stands hope; there stands hope,
Through the windows of my mind.

Upon the highways of life,
I've been lost 'n' found
And even turned around
Trying to track a lost dream down.

Without a dream in my heart,
Life makes me feel so out of place
When all the things I've hoped for
Pass before my face.

But through the windows of my mind
And the darkness that I find,
There stands hope; there stands hope,
Through the windows of my mind.

Lady-Lovesmith
(For Dorothy Sizemore Smith)

In the course of a lifetime,
You've been in my every school of thought
For your loving words of wisdom
Can never be sold or bought.

You are the goddess of love
Who teaches self-love and pride.
You are the voice of experience and reason
That pushed me up the mountainside.

With a touch of class and style,
You gave my heart a picture-perfect smile
That made living and learning
All the more worthwhile.

For ever since the days
And times of my youth,
You've been my undercurrent of strength
In my stream of consciousness and truth.

The Sweetheart Swindler

Like a careless driver behind the wheel,
He'll wine and dine you to death,
Blow your mind, and rob you blind
Of all the dreams you have left.
He never gives, but always receives
Because he's a smooth operator
With a sweetheart swindle up his sleeve.

He'll send you a rainbow of roses,
And be your full-time fool for fun,
Because he's a handsome heartless devil
Ready to make a hit and run.

Time after time
It just goes on and on
When Mr. Wright
Becomes Mr. Wrong.

His little loving ways are beyond
All shadows of a doubt
Until you really get hip
To what he's all about.

He'll send you a rainbow of roses
And be your fulltime fool for fun
Because he's a handsome heartless devil
Ready to make a hit and run.

Time after time
It just goes on and on
When Mr. Wright
Becomes Mr. Wrong.

His little loving ways are beyond
All shadows of a doubt
Until you really get hip
To what he's all about.

Don't get hooked on good looks
And sweet nothing impressions
Because all he wants is your hard
Earned cash and your prized possessions.

Like a Movin' Target

Just when I think I've made
A direct hit, your love becomes a movin'
Target. You're neither here nor there,
But in my heart you're everywhere.

Your mood of the moment
Can kill with kindness and still
Be unkind; 'Cause you're a livin'
Question mark at any given time.

Your love is like a movin' target,
and though we may be worlds apart,
I'm still aimin' for your heart.
Your love is like a movin' target.

I can't put my finger on it,
But I sure do adore, whatever
It is you do to me that keeps
Me comin' back for more.

I'll shoot my best shot
Whether right or wrong,
You've played hard to get much too long.
But my weaknesses have made me strong.

Your love is like a movin' target,
And though we may be world's apart,
I'm still aimin' for your heart.
Your love is like a movin' target.

First Impressions

First Impressions,
And love at first sight,
Can really ruin your whole life
When you find that you've hooked up
With the wrong Mr. Wright.

'Cause in this made-up, make believe
Game of real life, where all jokers
Are surely wild, picture-perfect smiles
Are just for style.

So I've been shooked, and I've been tooked,
I've been had, and I've been hooked
By the ugly egos behind pretty faces
And good looks.

Love Me, For Me

If you give of yourself
To a brand new start,

You can love me for me.
Straight from the heart.

No matter what we say or do,
There's no way we can know
All the things life will
Put us through.

So love me for me
And nothing less.
Love me for free
For I am love at its best.

I can't run and hide from myself,
And I can't begin
To pretend to be
Nobody else.

The price we pay
for a slice of life is too much to pay,
But where there's a will
I know that love will find a way.

So love me for me.
And nothing less.
Love me for free
For I am love at its best.

Miss Bad Little Honey

Miss Bad Little Honey,
Don't you know your love
Is finger licking good.
Miss Bad Little Honey,
I would like to make
You mine if I could.

Miss Bad Little Honey,
Yuz a bad little honey.

Sugar-dumpling,
Apple-pie,

Honey sweet,
You're the apple of my eye.

Sugardaddy,
Baby Ruth,
Good 'n' Plenty
Sweet-tooth.

Miss Bad Little Honey,
Don't you know your love
Is finger licking good.
Miss Bad Little Honey,
I would like to make
You mine if I could.

Miss Bad Little Honey,
Yuz a bad little honey.

Now and Later
Something-sweet
Chocolate-honey
What-a-treat.

Let God Be God
(For Sister Melinda Gaddy)

Let God Be God in His own way,
And His truth will be yours
Forever and a day
Let God Be God.

From everlasting to everlasting,
God is God all by himself.
For He, the Almighty,
Needs no help from nobody else.

Let God be God in His own way,
And His truth will be yours
Forever and a day.
Let God be God in His own way.

For always and forever, whatever

Your worldly troubles may be,
Let the Lord into your life,
And He will set you free.

Forever and ever, let Him lead you
The straight and narrow way.
He's the one and only God
That is yours forever and a day.

Let God be God
And His truth will be yours
Forever and a day.
Let God be God.

First Things First

First things first.
You're second to none
That's the way of the world
'Cause everybody's looking out
For number one.

Love Finds Its Own Way
(A Tribute to Gladys Knight & the Pips)

With every beat of my heart,
You're my one and only need to be
And for once in my life, you bring
Out the best in me.

Heaven-sent
And straight from above,
I was saved by the grace
Of your love.

Just be my lover
And save the overtime for me.
Its only a part-time love,
But I love you wholeheartedly.

You're the best thing that ever happened
To me, and that I can't deny,

For neither one of us wants to be
The first to say good-bye.

Because ain't no greater love
That's more than words can say,
And if that'll make you happy,
It's gotta be that way.

Heaven-sent,
And straight from above,
I was saved by the grace
Of your love.

Then Came You
(A Tribute to Phillipé Wynne and the Spinners)

I'm so glad you walked
Into my life. You're one of a kind,
And just as long as we have love,
I just can't get you off my mind.

You put the magic in the moonlight
Where there was none to be found.
I could never repay your love,
But I'll be around.

Wynne my way was all dark,
And cloudy through and through,
I felt the presence of a mighty love,
And then came you.

And as we live a little, laugh a little,
My love is truly yours in every way.
But they just can't stop it,
The games some people play.

Love don't love nobody,
So I've been told,
But just to be with you
Is a joy to behold.

Wynne my way was all dark
And cloudy through and through,
I felt the presence of a mighty love
And then came you.

Inflation*

Things might change,
And the tension might ease,
But ever since money put this country on its feet,
It was destined to return this country to its knees,
And now;

>The cost of living.......higher
>More people getting......fired
>Unemployment lines........longer
>The trend grows.......stronger

>**It's a very old way of destroying a nation,**
>It's called inflation.

Who enjoys watching prices score,
Or making less and paying more?
But at this rate, can we ever win?
Seems the more we do get,
The more we spend.
We could blame it on politics,
Like we so often do;
And of course it's the government's fault,
But this is our fault too.
You see everyday,

>The rich and the poor...dealing
>Most people busy...stealing
>We show little, or no...discretion
>Fanning the flames of...recession
>The economy boarders...starvation
>To sum it up in a word...inflation.

*Written with James F. Queen

His-Story*
(Part 1)

You don't have to listen to me,
The truth is there for all to see;
Read, his-story.

Sign for the elite force
For the most part you have no choice
You give him your body,
And he takes away your voice;
Separate to weaken; divide and defeat
Making the young to fight his battles,
Or he'll kill them in the street.
Ahh, there's war on the horizon'
For many more to die in;
More mothers will cry, and

*Written with James F. Queen

His-Story*
(Part 2)

Youngblood
In the name of those you love
What are you thinking of?
Read, you need to read.
Read, his-story.

War makes money,
Minus, the men;
If you've read it once
It's time you read it again.

Youngblood,
What are you thinking of?
Read, read, read,
Not yours, but his-story.

You don't have to listen to me,
The truth is there for all to see;
Read, his-story.

*Written with James F. Queen

Unless We Learn to Love*

The facts are all too clear
What we now hold dear
Is soon to disappear.

Unless we learn to love.

Flowers will cease to grow.
Mother Nature will close her show.
Peace will be no more.

Unless we learn to love.

There will be no starlit nights.
No more pleasant sight
Like the warm, sweet smile
Of a happy child.

Unless we learn to love.

You the rich
Who struggle for acclaim.
You the poor,
Who struggle for change;
All your struggling
Will be in vain.

Unless we learn to love.

It is our selfishness and moral lack
That we must rise above;
Oh people!, hate will surely destroy us.

—- Unless we learn to love.

*Written with James F. Queen

Act No. 1*

Acting on time.
Acting in time,
Only time will tell.
Acting with the sword of justice,
Or just acting to rebel.
Acting like there is no action
That isn't acting behind you;
Acting like the world should wait
Until your acting actions are through.
Acting actions of self-satisfaction,
And if acting was a fact;
The first act of acting real
Would be really not to act.

*Written with James F. Queen

Act No. 2*

Acting happy,
Acting sad,
That it's an act
Is just too bad.
Act on actor,
But before Act 2 is through
Re-evaluate.
Set the records straight,
Or Act 2 will be on you!%#&@+?

*Written with James F. Queen

Private Lines

They have given themselves the right
To bug everyone's phone;
And the Constitution is on ice
In parts unknown.
They tell us it's to stop conspiracy
And similar shady deals;
I say Hoover was a mother

With Webster hot on his heels.
There was a time when private lines
Were something we paid for and usually got.
Well, they left us with the lines;
It's just the privacy we have not.
They say it's for crime prevention,
Or in the interest of national security,
But if they were taking care of the nation,
Right,
Our homes would be left to you and me.
We've been told this type of thing
Only happens under dictators' rule;
Well, it sure looks like our leader
And the tyrannical rulers,
Went to the same damn schools.
So when in your home,
You use your phone
For business or just to call a friend,
Have no fear, but don't talk too clear
The FBI might be listening in.

Toys 'R' Us

In this game of real life
Where the naked truth is rarely told,
Don't be had by the playmate
Of remote control.

Like stuffed animals
In an asphalt city zoo
Plain Jane and John Doe
Are all a part of you.

Because in this land of the giants,
Mother Media is the 20th Century Fox
That winds us up like Gizmos 'n' Gadgets,
Tin soldiers, 'n' Jack in the Box.

And so Simple Simon says,
How do we spell relief from despair
When it seems we've come so far
To end up nowhere?

As our perfectly polite nonsense
Is somebody else's "In God We Trust"
And for the sake of surface thrills
Remote-controlled Toys "R" truly us.

Toyed with like human robots
Stigmatized and tranquilized
By the far-fetched freaks
Of free enterprise.

Like classic cartoon characters
At the end of a noose,
The invisible empire of power
Just won't turn us loose.

And so Simple Simon says,
How do we spell relief from despair
When it seems that we've come so far
To end up nowhere?

Yet our perfectly polite nonsense
Is somebody else's "In God We Trust"
And for the sake of surface thrills
Remote controlled Toys "R" truly us.

All Rights Reserved
(Part 1)

I'm gonna call
The Library of Congress
In Washington, D.C. and ask them
If they can copyright your love for me
'Cause I want all rights reserved.

And if in fact, true love
Speaks much louder than words,
I don't want anyone to steal
The melody of sweet-harmony from me
That my heart has always heard.

I want all rights reserved.
I need complete copyright control

To the sweet sensations of love,
Deeply rooted in your heart and soul.
I want all rights reserved.

I don't want no trespassin' backstabber
With his hands on private property
Or loitering with what belongs to me;
'Cause I'm sick and tired of being single and free.
I want all rights reserved.

All Rights Reserved
(Part 2)

For if you should ever become
The proud possession of the public domain,
It would push me somewhat off the wall
And drive me damn near insane.

I'm so sincerely
In love with you
That a common law
Copyright just won't do.

You're my number one melody
On the best seller's list
Of my life. You're my precious,
Priceless Paradise.

And I want all rights reserved.
I need complete copyright control
To the sweet sensations of love
Deeply rooted in your heart 'n' soul.
I want all rights reserved.

Chocolate City Candy

Just a taste of you
Makes my life so complete
Learnin' to love you
Is a special treat.

The little lovin' things you do
Forever makes you honey sweet,
Your Good 'N' Plenty lovin'
Just knocks me off my feet.

You're my Sugar Baby
Peppermint-Pattie Pearl
My M&M Plain, Chocolate City
Candy Girl.

My lifetime, Life Saver
Fifth Avenue, Lover's Lane Park
My Butterfingered, whatchamacallit
Such sweetness in the dark.

Now and later you'll always
Be my Mary Jane, my Baby Ruth
My Mounds of Almond Joy
Chocolate honey sweet tooth.

Let me be your Payday
Sugar Daddy galore,
Your 100 Grand
Mr. Goodbar for sure.

When you turn on your total
Tootsie Roll charm,
Your chocolate cherry kisses
Make me melt in your arms.

You're my Sugar Baby,
Peppermint-Pattie Pearl.
My M&M Plain, Chocolate City
Candy Girl.

The Grace of Faith

A high on the grace of faith
Will take you to the sky
On a heavenly high, hold fast
To hopes 'n' dreams, don't let
Them pass you by.

A natural high on faith
Will set your spirit free
And give you a taste of grace
From faith's learnin' tree.

Discover the Lord God
And your wounded soul
Will bleed no more. You will
Find the words of wisdom that you've
Been looking for.

Dream on through the undreamable
Love on through the unliveable
Live on through the unloveable
And the love of the Lord will
Take you higher on the grace
Of faith....

South Africa: The Cesspool
(A Tribute to Nelson Mandela)

South Africa is the last cesspool
Of white minority domination,
And I'm telling you now, it's a funky situation.

The so-called economic sanction
Against Botha's regime
Is just another automatic, bureaucratic smokescreen.

The quiet diplomacy of destructive
Engagement has been given a second wind
Because the cowboy who runs the country
Wants us to think that Apartheid is our friend.

South Africa is the last cesspool
Of white minority domination.
And I'm telling you now, it's a funky situation.

The price of black South Africa's
Freedom will never be free
While the executive cowboy Klansman
Puts on the whole armor of white supremacy.

Divide and Conquer
That's the name of the game
For the warm ties between Pretoria
And Washington are one and the same.

And until the backs of the powers
That be, are up against the wall
Limited sanctions are really no sanction at all.

Because South Africa is the last cesspool
Of white minority domination
And I'm telling you now, it's a funky situation.

Apartheid
(A Tribute to Winnie Mandela)

When black South Africans
And non-whites only exist
On refugee reservations,
Townships or hopeless homelands.

What do you have?
The immoral unjustifiable
High of white South African
Apartheid.

Apartheid is the legendary livin' proof
Of white-washed truths that perpetuate
White South Africa's police state of
Racial supremacy and a racial hate.

From South Carolina Jim Crow
To South African Apartheid
The handwriting's on the wall
'Cause there has never been equality
With liberty and justice for all.

So what do you have?
Apartheid.

Jesus Paid the Cost

When Jesus died
On the cross,
He made a way
For a world that was lost.

He paid in full for the sins
Of the world thereof
With the great goodness
Of His love.

Jesus paid the cost
To set me free.
When He died on Calvary,
Jesus paid the cost.

He paid with His blood
Through His sacrifice,
So that we might be born
Again in the newness of life.

I'm a child
Of the family of man,
But my soul's salvation
Is in my Savior's hand.

Jesus paid the cost
To set me free.
When He died on Calvary,
Jesus paid the cost.

Pain

Pain knows no one form
Pain is power over all nature kind.
Pain is giving birthright to new birth.
Pain is a brother climbing Mr. Jim Crow's wall.
Pain is hell if the brother starts to fall.
But, death knows no pain.

Time

Be not sad nor pensive
That time has taken the best
Of one's livelihood.
All shall be bound at a future
Day with a chain of years and
A ball of circumstance for life.

'Natural High'

On the wings of love
I get high. High naturally
When you're close to me.
And as all things in time
Do unfold, sweet sensations of love
Ignite my heart 'n' soul
To a natural high on happiness.

When You Give of Yourself

When from the depths
Of your inner being
You freely give of yourself,
Your free-spirited soul
Will find a home in the heart
Of someone else.

For the language of love
Becomes poetry in motion,
When you give of yourself
Through love and devotion.

'Cause the best things
In love and life are truly free,
When you give your heart
Through love so naturally.

On the Wings of Success
(An Ode to the Majestic Eagles)

When we put God first
Family second and business third
Up under the wings of love
Faith is the natural password.

And just as every road
Has a fork or a bend,
The majestic eagle is air born
On the wings of the wind.

To cling to a Raye of hope
On the wings of a positive theme
Is to soar like an ebony eagle
On the wings of self-esteem.

With the spirit of love and faith
As the key to our economic quest,
We can fly higher together
On the wings of sweet success.

And to soar like an eagle
On the wings of life, while in quest
Is to do all that we can do,
And let God do the rest.

Self-Service

All you got to do
Is serve yourself
Don't aspire to be
A star for somebody else,
Just serve yourself.

You got to know with your heart
What it takes to survive,
You must conceive, and believe
What it means to keep a dream alive.

Serve yourself
If you can conceive,
Why not believe?
And if you believe,
Faith will help you to achieve
Self-service.

Thankful Thinkin'

Our world stands on the edge
Of fate, and I really hope it's not too late
To color our world with hopes 'n' dreams
Of smilin' on tomorrow.

With Eyes of A Child

With eyes of a child
We're just grown up kids
Wearin' our heads upside down
Always smilin' through a frown.

I hope it's not too late
To put our heads on straight.
Why live through fixed false impressions?
Why not generate true love expressions?

Sound Experience

Bein' kool is OK,
But kool alone just can't stand
On its own behind the mask
Without common sense and class.

Everybody Has a Dream

Those of us who dream too much
Are just as bad as those who
Refuse to dream at all. For everyone
Should have a dream in their heart
No matter how big or small.

Family

If home is where the heart is,
Home grown love is true harmony at heart.
'Cause I've found the spirit of faith
In the fruit of the family tree.
And we are forever one family
...through faith.

The Only Heaven I Know

I may never get to heaven
Feeling the way I do.
The only heaven I know
Is wrapped up in you.

The womb of your love
Warms my heart to no end.
You're a fresh breath of life
To a lifetime friend.

When I'm in your warm
And tender embrace,
There's no place
That I'd rather be,
'Cause being with you
Is simply heaven to me.
The only heaven I know.

Marriage Can Be a Monster

Ain't no if's, ands 'n' but's about it
Truckloads of lovin' can be tons of fun,
But marriage can be a monster,
If you make it one.

Fussin' 'n' fightin',
Do or die...
Wills 'n' won't...
Talkin' 'bout your do's 'n' don't's.

Misplaced mixed emotions
Got your mind in a maze
When you said "I do,"
You must have been in a daze.

Inlaws are outlaws
And as livin' proof,
You're married to each other's family
'Cause somebody's lyin' on the truth.

It ain't enough beauty
In this sweet-bitter-beast.
No justice in the peace of mind
That you find, you were simply love blind.

Ain't no if's 'n' but's about it
Truckloads of lovin' can be tons of fun,
But marriage can be a monster,
If you make it one.

1600 Pennsylvania Avenue

You didn't choose us, we chose you;
So let's be clear on exactly who chose whom.
That we are victims of a double standard of living,
Not even you will deny.
That it does exist is not the question;
Nor is the question why.
You make promises behind our backs,
Although they are against our will.
You give away millions, while we foot the bill.
You make laws to correct laws
Each with its own built-in clause,
And you fancy yourself important
To the sound of your own applause.
You tell us we can't own a damn thing
Unless taxes we give.
You tax the right to die as well as the right to live.
You shelter a few as you misrepresent the rest;
And it has been your misrepresentation,
That has us in this mess.
We put you there to do a job,

And as it seems you are not the right man.
We demand you call a press conference
With resignation in hand.
This could be sent to many officials,
And it would still be true;
Only this time it's to somebody's boss
At 1600 Pennsylvania Avenue.

Blue-Eyed Booty

Bedroom blue eyes
Sweet-nothings in a catcall
A taste of the forbidden fruit
And the taboo of it all.

Blonde blue-eyed soul
At any perverse price
Is surely some brothers'
Private paradise.

Somehow enough
Is never enough
Of that blue-eyed
Sweet funky stuff.

And some sisters sense
Of magic in the moonlight
Is in the arms of massa
White knight.

Blue-eyed brickhouse
Or a simple plain Jane
If her booty is blonde,
You'll love her just the same.

And somehow enough
Is never enough
Of the blue-eyed
Sweet funky stuff.

But take heed to your own
And those of your kind

Learn to love who you are
And the ties that bind.

The centerfold of the *Penthouse*
May be a real Miss America cutey
But you don't have to stoop
To somebody else's standard of beauty.

No Cream in the Coffee

Thanks, but no thanks!
No cream in the coffee
For me. I'll take mine
Just natural and cream free.

Brown sugar in my coffee
Without cream is just fine
Because their taster's choice
Is theirs and not mine.

It's not prejudice,
It's the pride
That makes me feel
The way I do deep down inside.

They say times have changed
And tables have turned, but
There'll be no cream in my coffee
As far as I'm concerned.

I don't want or need
Nobody else's cream of the crop
Because I've got a coffeemate
That's good to the very last drop.

It's not prejudice,
It's the pride
That makes me feel
The way I do deep down inside.

Blue-Black Honey
(Dark Obsession)

Miss Blue-Black Honey
Of pure Ebony Gold
Lady love of the sun
Only you can make me whole.

And from the very heart
Of my blue-black pearl,
I found a sacred soulmate
In a Dark 'N' Lovely Girl.

My Dark Obsession,
She's love in living color.
My prize possession,
I could never love another.

Two black hearts
One of a kind
Dark 'N' Lovely
Midnight sunshine.

Lady of my love
One and only one
Spirit in the dark
Second to none.

My Dark Obsession,
She's love in living color
My prize-possession,
I could never love another.

Every Day is Mother's Day

Every day is Mother's Day in my heart
Because she taught me to be my own best friend
Gave me a sense of pride within,
And I just feel like I've been born again.
Through childhood fears, frustrations and
Failures I fought, and I give thanks
To you Mama for you were the breadwinner

Of my food for thought.
You are the goddess of great goodness
That conquers my soul in every part
Because each and every day is Mother's Day in my heart.
In the name of love,
Mama, my heart belongs to you.
'Cause you kept my every dream alive,
And you made the impossible come true.
The creative source of your soul
Is intensive care thereof, for you are
The first lady in the perfect majesty of motherly love.
You are the goddess of great goodness
That conquers my soul in every part
Because each and every day is Mother's Day in my heart.

Some Christians

Don't stand on the words
Of someone else,
Know the Lord and Savior
For Yourself.

Stand up for Christ;
Don't be no sugar-coated Christian
Living a lie for life.
Stand up for Christ.

Some come to church to mind
Everybody's business but their own.
While others only come to leave
Their religion at home.

Some come to pray
Louder than loud,
While others only come
To be with the in crowd

Some come to see
While others come to be seen;
Some come to play church
And cry holy if you know what I mean.

Some come to be happy
While others come to be gay
'Cause the Holy Spirit don't come
'Til the music starts to play.
So let us take heed
To what the Word really has to say.

Stand up for Christ;
Don't be no Sunday morning saint
Living a lie for life,
Stand up for Christ.

The Father's Day Poem
(King of Hearts)

When your heart stands at attention
Because love called your name,
You are forever the King of Hearts
Of the faithful father's hall of fame.

Just when I thought
I couldn't be strong,
You gave me the will
To right what was wrong.

For the love and understanding
That you never fail to give,
You are the king of all hearts
Who has ever lived.

And now after all's been
Said and done,
I just want you to know
You're still a special someone.

Information Is Power
(A Tribute to Dick Gregory)

When you know who you are
And it's fully understood,
The power of information
Can do nothing but good.

To be in the know, you don't have
To live in a highrise ivory tower.
Knowledge is a priceless pearl
Of wisdom and information is power.

No time to give up, or give in
'Cause you've been shook.
Opportunity is all around you,
If you only knew where to look.

As knowledge is food for thought
To the fully-hungry mind,
The eyes of information
Are forever sight to the blind.

So now is the time
And this is the hour,
Money and education are fine,
But information is power.

In the school of life, intellectual
Liberation will help you stay the course,
For the power of information is life's
Greatest natural resource.

Knowledge is information
Under color-conscious control.
Information is power
Sometimes bought and sold.
Knowledge is information
More precious than gold.

To stay on time and in tune
With that inner voice,
A true knowledge of self will help
You make the right choice.

To live and learn is a life-line
To the lowly livin' dead.
Information is power to see
What's in the back of your head.

For now is the time,
And this is the hour.
Money and education are fine,
But information is power.

A Raye of Hope
(A Tribute to John Raye)

Like midnight sunshine
Through deep darkness and despair,
The power of your inner spirit
Is always there.

High on the wings of life
In an upward bound,
You are a Raye of love's joy
That takes us to higher ground.

The warm thoughts
Of the sunshine in your heart
Bring those together
Who were worlds apart.

With the creative consciousness
Of the majestic Eagle and J.R.A.,
You are the timeless hopes
Of a new and brighter day.

The way you give of yourself
Is so simply divine,
You are a Raye of love who makes
Us high on sunshine.

You are an eaglenomical earthquake
Our anchor, and our guide
A Raye of hope for the helpless
A portrait of African-American pride.

'The Dark Side of a Star'

Somebody blew a bubble
And a star was born. She was

Riding on the wings of the wind
Until she tasted Hollywood's bitter end.

She was born a star
In her heart, yes it's true
That the well-to-do wonders of Hollywood
Have broken her heart in two.

Success is a minefield
Of hang ups, let downs, and setbacks
All wrapped up in the game
Of fortune and fame.

In Hollywood
Everybody trips on gold dust
With false fixed expressions
To fill their cup. Nobody seems
To know just how high is up.

But through the maze of magic dreams
And miracles, expect the unexpected.
When reachin' for a star, trust in the truth,
And be just who and what you are.

_____'s Love

Someway, someday, somehow,
I'll be your blessing in disguise
Like a genie from outta nowhere,
I'll appear right before your very eyes.

Becuz my love for you is so deep
That it cuts like a knife
Through all pain, misery and strife,
Just to give to you the gift of
My love for life.

Now I may not be a world-famed
Shining super star
Or ride in a custom-made fancy car, but the
Likes of my love for you is so
Much better by far.

And though I don't have money
Or expensive gifts to give out
At will. When you trust in the
Treasures of _____'s love, you
Gonna know just how I feel.

Becuz my love for you is so deep
That it cuts like a knife
Through all pain, misery and strife,
Just to give to you the gift of
My love for life........._____'s love.

How Do I Say 'Thank You'?

How do I show appreciation
For your grace from beginning to end?
How can I show my gratitude
Over and over again?

How can I find the words
To take my heart to mind?
How do I find a way to say
I'm laying my feelings on the line?

How do I say thank you for making me see
All that I needed to be?
How do I say thank you
For lighting the torch of my destiny?

What could I possibly
Say in honor of you
That would say thanks
For my dreams come true?

How do I say you gave me
A new vision of hope for tomorrow?
How do I say you've been my strength
Where there was so much pain and sorrow?

How do I say thank you for making me see
All that I needed to be?
How do I say thank you

For being a part of me?
How do I say "Thank you"?

Only Always

If you wanna know
How long am I gonna
Love you, all I can simply
Say is only always.

Only always
Will I be lovin' you
For days on end; and only always
Am I gonna be your lifetime friend
When you need someone to believe in
Only always
Just as long as we
Share love and care
For each other, only always
Can there be love in our hearts
For one another.

Only always and forever
Will I leave you never
And if you ever feel you need
Someone to be your backbone
Lean on me and you'll never
Walk alone—for only always

A Poet of the People

I am a writer of rhyme
And Reason
A poet of Sound and Sense
For all seasons.

I am not afraid
To take a stand
My only weapon
Is my pen in hand.

Yes, I am the keeper of all time
A revolution of the mind.

Yes, I am a poet
A poet.
A poet,
A poet of the people.

I am the life of a people's
Long lost sense of pride
I am the hopes and dreams
Locked away deep down inside.

I am the way with words
Like the ancient griot
I am the language of love's
Epic hero.

Yes, I am a poet
A poet,
A poet,
A poet of the people.

I am not afraid
To take a stand
My only weapon
Is my pen in hand.

I am the keeper of all time
A revolution of the mind.

A poet of the people.

Don't Add Loss to Loss
(A Tribute to Mr. Joe Louis Dudley)

When subtracting the joy
From the pain
It adds up to a gift of spirit
No one can explain.

Come what may
Nobody's born to lose
As long as you're livin'
The choice is yours to choose.

A man with the knowledge
The wisdom, and the will
Is a man with the fuller spirit
And a faith made of steel.

No matter what people might say
Today was tomorrow yesterday
And no matter what the cost
Don't add loss to loss.

To live and love
In a fuller state of mind
Is to give of yourself
One day at a time.

In the light of divine order
Any lost cause can be found
And because of the inner you
You know there's a higher ground.

To make you feel brand new
Is to fill your lovin' cup
So the gift of a good challenge
Can show you which way is up.

Don't live your life
On what was, way back when
Pick yourself up, and you can
Soar to sweet success again.

No matter what people might say
Today was tomorrow yesterday
And no matter what the cost
Don't add loss to lost.

Pride and Joy
(A Tribute to Marvin Gaye)

When Love Comes Knocking At Your Heart
With All That It Can Bring
That's the Way Love Is Because
Ain't Nothing Like The Real Thing.

You're Such A Stubborn Kind Of Fellow
That You're Love's Native Son
You're My Pride and Joy, And I'll Be Doggone
If You Ain't A Wonderful One.

And Ain't that Peculiar How Love Woke Me Up
This Morning From Out of The Blue
Yet How Sweet It Is
To Be Loved By You.

The Feeling of Sexual Healing Is Never Enough
Because You Got To Give It Up To Be Strong
So Come Get To This
And Let's Get It On.

If I Could Build My Whole World
Around You, Your Precious Love
Would Be The Bottom Line
If This World Were Mine.

I Heard It Through The Grapevine
That We've Come To The End Of Our Road,
But I'll Be Your Strength In Love
To Help You Carry The Load.

You're Such A Stubborn Kind Of Fellow
That You're Love's Native Son
You're My Pride And Joy, And I'll Be Doggone
If You Ain't A Wonderful One.

The Moody Booty Blues
(An Aid for AIDS)

Some like 'em short; Some like 'em tall
Some like 'em big; Some like 'em small
Some like 'em hairy; Some like 'em bald
Some like 'em any way they cum, skinny legs 'n' all.

And if you like 'em fat
You can get a truckload
Of that, or if you like 'em slim
That's some pretty good trim.

Be they black, white,
Chicano or Greek.
If you must have a ready made
Freak for everyday in the week.

Make it your business
To know with whom you'll be
Dippin' and dabbin'
And end up crabbin'
In the dead sea of V.D.

So stop, live, listen, and learn
Before its your turn
To get burned by love's tender trap
For when you fall into the gap of some
Unknown nudey, just remember
These words of heed 'bout love's loose booty.

A Prayer

Though some things in life
Are neither here nor there
I plan to stay a believer
In the power of prayer, for
We all have our crosses
To bear.

Forever Somebody

I often find myself
Left out in the cold,
But still there burns
A spark in the deep
Darkness of my heart.

And I know that I'm forever somebody
To search and find an inner peace
Is to search and find somebodiness.

My yester-dream has passed with time
Tomorrow's dreams cling fast to mind.
Because I am somebody
I am forever somebody.

A Message to Michael
(Too Bad To Be Good)

Now is the time to take
Another thriller off the shelf
You've got the mystery magic
So go on with your bad self.

Everything you touch
Is a masterpiece
Musically speaking
To say the least.

You were born to be a starchild
From the very first start
And like the Peter Pan man
You face life with a childish heart.

But you can't afford to forget
When you do what you do
'Cause young minds look up
To the image of you.

So from bad to worse
You're too bad to be good

For unlike storybook children
You never had a childhood.

Whether off the wall
Or simply misunderstood
You've got it bad
And that ain't good.

Your bad-body language
Is bigger than life so I'm told
And unlike sister Janet you're
Completely out of control.

If some things are private
Then let it be so,
But don't put us in a state
Of shock looking like a scarecrow.

At the wrong end of the rainbow
I see the reflection of a falling star
Your ever-changing face value
Won't let you be who you are.

When you're lost 'n' found
And then lost again
The make-up of the man
In the mirror is wearing thin.

Though your sense-of-self,
And cultural-pride is numb,
You can't afford to forget
Just where you come from.

What I'm saying may seem somewhat
Off the wall or simply strange,
But believe me brother, "You got to
Make that change...."

Let's Make a Baby
(The Tree of Life)

The language of love
Can't begin to explain
The love and commitment
The pleasure and the pain.

A child of the sun
Fruit of the womb
The tree of life
In full bloom.

So let's make a baby
And call it love
With divine blessings
From heaven above
Let's make a baby
And call it love.

The womb of the mind
And body must be one
To bring forth a Godchild
Of life that second's to none.

To give breath of life
To Mother Nature's pearl
Is to give birthright
To a brand new world.

A sacred sensation
Is a new-born birth
A co-creator with God
Simply heaven on earth.

So let's make a baby
And call it love
With divine blessing
From heaven above
Let's make a baby
And call it sweet love.

Long Live The Memory

As I journey
Through this broken heart of love,
Long live the memory
Of the sunshine we shared.

And as I stroll the deep dark corridors
Of my mind's heart and soul,
Long live the memory
Of our hopes and dreams
For they shall never grow old.

Long live the memory
Of our happiness to be
Because I truly love you
I search my soul for the part
Of you that lives in me.

Long live the memory
Of how you set me free
From the pains of loneliness
And the chains of misery.

Long love the kiss of love's
Magic touch that always meant
So much, intensive love and care,
And to this first-class friendship
That we've spared, long live the memory
Of love's treasured pleasure
That we've shared.
Long live the memory....

It Ain't What Ya Know
(It's Who Ya Know)
(Part I)

Who ya know
Can make a way
Out of no way 'cause that's
The game that people play.

When nobody knows
Your name, who ya know
Can be the key to your
Claim to fame.

It ain't what ya know
But it's who ya know,
And it just goes to show
It ain't always what ya know.

Don't fool yourself
Into livin' a lie. Don't go
For what ya know, when what
Ya know don't apply.

Where ya comin' from
Will make ya stumble and fall,
When what ya thinkin'
Ain't where it's at at all.

It ain't what ya know,
But it's who ya know
And it just goes to show
It ain't always what ya know.

What Color Was Jesus?
(A Tribute to Rev. Willie F. Wilson & UTBC)

Let the spirit of truth
Color you higher
In His divine-holiness
Jesus was the black Messiah.

If the naked truth
Is the living-light,
There ain't no way
Jesus could have been white.

Mother Mary was a Sister-Lady
Jesus was a Brother-Man
Now what color was Jesus?
Tell me, if you think you can

What color was Jesus?
Jesus was a black man.

Michelangelo changed the world
With a lovable white-lie
And our sacred slice of life
Was only pie in the sky.

But a white-washed truth
Is like no truth at all
For truth crushed to earth
Will still stand tall.

Mother Mary was a Sister-Lady
Jesus was a Brother-Man
Now what color was Jesus?
Tell me, if you think you can
What color was Jesus?
Jesus was a black man.

Without self knowledge
Self-love and mutual trust
Everybody seems to know
Who we are except us.

The fact that Jesus was black
Is simply wholly taboo
But the truth is on its way
And too long overdue.

Times: 19 and 29

So many people scufflin'
Trying to have enough, and
Things are just that rough 'cause

Time ain't been this hard
Since 19 and 29.
You know, time ain't been this hard,
Since 19, 19 and 29.

You don't need a great "economic" mind
To know a dollar-bill, ain't worth a dime,
And with long unemployment lines
There's bound to be a rise in crime.
And to quote the words of a friend of mine;

Times ain't been this hard
Since 19 and 29
Ahhh, he said, times ain't been this hard
Since 19, 19 and 29.

Got good folks lyin', old folks crying;
Everybody's telling,
But the sellers ain't buying;
And just the other day, I heard a man say:
It's one sure sign
When scotch drinkers, start drinking wine.

That times ain't been this hard
Since 19, 19 and 29.

And to quote the words, of a friend of mine:
"If I had the soup, I'd start a line;

'Cause times ain't been this hard since
19, 19, 19 and 29
19 and 29."

Love Don't Live By Sex Alone

For those who're players
Glamor girls are baby dolls.
Just as pretty boys 'n' good hair
Will surely make some women stop 'n' stare.

But when lost in lust for love
Beauty's only skin deep,
Just as uglyness is to the bone
Cuz in truth, love don't live by sex alone.

A man of the world
Caught up in the loose booty
Of bed and board's touch and go

Will find it nearly impossible to give
Love a chance to grow.

So I'm putting it down to the way I feel
Without the intensive bed time thrills
Of high society's sex appeal.
Love is a taste of honey that stands on its own
Becuz in life, love don't live by sex alone.

Everybody's Out Ta Lunch
(Food for Thought)

As life becomes
One dark dull 'n' dingy dream
In search of the things thought to be hip
Everybody's out ta lunch on some kinda trip.

Half-hearted hang-ups
Have made you a mortal felony
And the untouchable powers that be
Will never set you free from poverty.

Everybody's out ta lunch
Bloodthirsty, moneyhungry humanhounds
Have turned the world upside down.
And everybody's out ta lunch.

Just like soap operas
And fairytales
All lust and no love
Has become a real thrill.

Educated fools, cannibals
And fatcats of the power play
Are all political actors
Of the greatest show on earth today.

Everybody's out ta lunch
Bloodthirsty, moneyhungry, humanhounds
Have turned the world upside down
And everybody's out ta lunch.

I Am Because God Is...

Because of the God force
Within me, He is mine and I am His,
For I am what I am
All because God is...

God is my heavenly father.
From up on high and above,
He is the light of all life
In the spirit of heavenly love.

When I find that I am in need
Of heaven's intensive love and care,
I just bow my head
And whisper a prayer.

And when life suddenly smiles
Upon me with a frown,
And all my ups start to look down,
I put my trust in God because He is always around.

My God is forever mine,
As I am eternally His,
For I am what I am
All because God is....

Hot Line to Heaven

Twenty-four hours a day
The hotline to heaven
Up above is still wide
Open for your love.

No matter when
What, or where,
Don't despair, you can always
Call Him up through prayer.

And it won't cost you
One single dime to call
On Him when you need
Some peace of mind.

Twenty-four hours a day
The Hot Line to Heaven
Up above is still wide
Open for your love.

When you call on the Lord,
He'll never put you on hold
'Cause He's never too busy to
Save a lost soul.

And you don't need
Directory assistance
To get through, but keep the faith
And God will surely answer you.

'Cause twenty-four hours a day
The Hot Line to Heaven up above
Is still wide open for your
Love.

Deep and Quiet Love

Can I be your deep and quiet
Love, your cream of the crop?
I'm hooked on your love,
And I just can't stop.

When something's a burning
Deep in my heart's desire,
There just ain't no smoke
Without fire.

You're the girl of my dreams
My sweet-honey-brown.
You're the melody of my life,
And I'm lovin' you the second time around.

When the newness is gone
For you, I'm born again
And forever happy to be
Your intimate friend.

From me to you,
Your wish is my command
Maybe I'm a fool to love you,
But it's out of my hands.

Because when somethin's a burning
Deep in my heart's desire,
There just ain't no smoke
Without fire.

Soul in the Super Bowl
(A Tribute to Doug Williams and the Washington Redskins)

As another myth is shattered,
Let the truth forever unfold
Because the brother truly gave
Of himself in the Super Bowl.

For in this game of real life,
A Mastermind of the darker hue
Was the MVP of Super Soul Bowl
Number Twenty-two.

When the Skins were down by ten,
It was the beginning of the end.
Then they were up by forty-two,
And suddenly the Broncos were through.

Doug is the Jackie Robinson
Of America's NFL.
He did what he had to do
In grand style, and he did it well.

But there's so much more
To Doug Williams the man
Than the first black Super Bowl
Quarterback with a pigskin in his hand.

For all of our unsung heroes
And sheroes of years gone past,
Doug is the essence of untapped
Potential with a touch of class.

So with all the hysterical
Historical inspiration galore,
Doug is the only brother who
Had the chance to even the score.

And in truth, Doug Williams is the
Jackie Robinson of America's NFL,
He did what he had to do
In grand style, and he did it well.

Everybody's Somebody's Fool
(Undercover Playmate)

Wild but peaceful,
So wonderfully warm,
You raged in my life
Like a secret storm.

We had a good thing going
Until who knows what went bad,
Now I find myself missing
Somethin' I never had.

It's too bad you belong
To somebody else,
I'm your part-time playmate,
And I just can't help myself.

Lovin' and being loved
Is simply joy divine,
But when will you be
Forever mine?

You got my mind in a maze.
My heart's in a noose.
You got me where you want me,
And I just can't turn you loose.

Something' you got
Keeps me livin' a lie,
I'm your secret sugar daddy
Your old stand by.

Behind closed doors,
Your part time lover,
Your full time fool,
Too hot to handle,
This undercover cool.

And as I live to learn,
I'm no exception to the rule.
For in affairs of the heart,
Everybody's somebody's fool.

The wisdom of a fool
Is sweet insanity undercover,
But I love you too much
To give you up to another.

Where there's smoke,
A so-called used to be
Can be the object of desire,
And even the best of strangers
Can light each others' fire.

The bond between you, him
And your children is ever strong,
But bein' the fool I am,
You keep me stringin' along.

Your undercover passion
Is nicer than nice,
But you belong to somebody else.
I'm livin' in a fool's paradise.

When all that's old
Is still brand new,
The question is...
Who's foolin' who?

And as I live to learn,
I'm no exception to the rule,
For in affairs of the heart
Everybody's somebody's fool.

The Epic Hero
(A Tribute to Michael Jackson)

Say, say, say
It's your Hallelujah Day.
Yet you've just begun,
But still you're such a lovely one.

You're such a rhythm child,
You and Billie Jean, but don't
Blame it on the Boogie 'cause
You're the dancing machine.

With the gift of song
In your heart and soul,
The way you move and groove
It's like remote control.

Startin' somethin'
Is your claim to fame,
And if they can't beat it
Who's to blame?

Like no one
I've ever seen
Or heard, you're an epic hero
In every sense of the word.

Working day and night
And going places can be rough,
But don't stop 'til you get
Enough.

When we rock with you
Your body language says it all,
'Cause that's the thriller magic
That keeps us dancing right off the wall.

You're such a rhythm child,
You and Billie Jean, but don't
Blame it on the Boogie 'cause
You're the dancing machine.

The Graduation Poem
(*Be the Best*)

Be The Best
And nothin' less
'Cause nothin' succeeds
Like sweet success.
Be The Best.

Whenever you do
What you do, when
You do it, faith
Will help you get through it.

Be your own best friend
And the super star in your
Own show. Believe in yourself
And go for what you know.

You are the future fruit
Of life's learnin' tree.
And in all you do, you've got
To be the best you can be.

Every endless new beginnin'
Is a brand-new fresh start,
When you, believe in you, deep
Down in your heart.

Say NO to Drugs
(Inspired by the tragic death of Len Bias)

A brainchild of life
Made of beautiful things 'n' stuff
A gold-nugget of pride
A rare diamond in the rough.

And there ain't no need
To sleep and wake up dead
When there's so much more
To live for instead.

So...Just Say No!

Say no to drugs, say no to dope
Say yes to life, say yes to hope
Say no to the same old bad news
Say no to deadly drugs and booze.

Just Say NO
Say NO to Drugs.

Babies Making Babies

Some kids are just a pain
Morning, night, and noon.
Some kids never grow up.
Others grow up all too soon.

With a new birth in her arms,
And another at her side,
They're all that she has
To give her a sense of pride.

Stop this wheel of shame.
Stop this wheel of pain.
Baby ain't got no name.
Don't know who's to blame.

Babies making babies.
Where do we draw the line?
Babies having babies.
It's a sign of the times.
Babies making babies.

You say when you get that feeling,
You just got to do it.
But oh, let me tell you child
In real life there's so much more to it.

And whether it's a lovable lad
Or a priceless baby girl,
This ain't no cabbagepatch kid
You're bringing into the world.

When it comes to life and love,
Tell me why can't you see
That love carries with it
A sense of pride and responsibility.

Hooked on the labor of love,
You gave into a feeling unknown.
And after motherhood the hard way,
You know, love don't live by sex alone.

Stop this wheel of shame.
Stop this wheel of pain.
Baby ain't got no name.
Don't know who's to blame.

Babies making babies.
Where do we draw the line?
Babies having babies.
It's a sign of the times.
Babies making babies.

Endangered Species

The ugly ego of self-hate
Is sin sick sadness.
Chocolate City's gone crazy.
We gotta stop the madness.

Everybody's out to ta lunch
On a crackedhead high.
We gotta stop the violence
And stop livin' a lie.
Black on black death
Is at an all-time high.

Young hustlers die young
Thinkin' its the only way.
Oozie City, war zone on
Any street U.S. of A.

Everybody's got an AK-47 rifle,
An AR-15 or a bloody knife.

Too uncaring to care.
No respect for life.

Programmed for a fate
Of failure. Nevertheless
By materialistic surface thrills
And only symbols of success.

Gold chains, designer clothes
BMW's and a Mercedes Benz,
Easy money, big money, fast livin'
Young hustlers...Dead end.

The object of extinction,
Public enemy number one.
An endangered species,
Mother Africa's native son.
Made of a pure black gold,
But, programmed to self-destruct
By remote control.

The ugly ego of self-hate
Is such sin sick sadness.
Chocolate City's gone crazy.
We gotta stop the madness.

Dealers of death and destruction
Are the heroes to our ghetto youth.
For they are the fruit of promise.
Teach the children the truth.

That old slave mentality
Is a plantation of the mind.
Second-hand self value
Is self destruction by design.

But for the love of our people,
No matter, a sister or a brother.
We gotta stand together
And fight for one another.

The most endangered
Species in all the earth
Is the new Bald Eagle
Black-balled from birth.

The lack of self-love
Self-respect, and hue-man pride
Is the cause and effect
Of black on black homicide.

The ugly ego of self-hate
Is sin sick sadness.
Chocolate City's gone crazy.
We gotta stop the madness.

From A Friend to A Friend

You're the gift of true love
That keeps right on giving.
You're my special wonder
That makes my life worth living.

And from a friend to a friend

If going through the motions
Make you feel like dirt,
Let me love away the pain.
Tell me where it hurts.

From a friend to a friend

Lay your head on my shoulder.
Lay your heart in my hand.
I'll be there when you need
A trusting heart to understand.

And from a friend to a friend
You've been my breath of life
In my every uphill climb.
You're a touch of class
In the course of a lifetime.

From a friend to a friend.

From No-Hope to New-Hope
(For Rev. Willie F. Wilson & UTBC)

A brighter tomorrow
Is calling our name,
A lost legacy of love
Must be reclaimed.

When we know who we are
Everbody is a star.
And from No-Hope to New-Hope,
I know we can cope.

It may not be convenient,
But ain't no-need to worry.
Because as quiet as it's kept,
It's so very necessary.

And now is the time
To take a stand.
There's a tower of power
In the palms of our hand.

The key to self-love
Is so simply divine.
And all we got to do
Is unlock our minds.

It may not be convenient,
But ain't no need to worry.
Because as quiet as it's kept,
It's so very necessary.

When we know who we are
Everybody is a star.
And from No-Hope to New-Hope,
I know we can cope.

Where Will My People Be?

I often think of the old times
When our fathers were beaten,
And our mothers stood crying.

Oh, how awful it must have been
To be brought to this place,
And sold as slaves to an inhuman race.

Working the fields of cotton, sugar, and corn
And begging for mercy
From the day they were born.

Getting no rest and having no fun
From the dawn of the morning
To the setting of the sun.

Oh Jesus, they prayed would help them someday
And take them back
To their homes far away.

Were the prayers they said all in vain?
For are we not slaves
With a different name?

To this thing called a man, have we not been loyal
To care for his sick or
To die in his wars?

But no longer will we come to your kissing feet,
While our women are raped,
While our children are beaten.

If war is the answer, then so it must be.
We care not for bloodshed,
But to be free.

If in it I'm killed, I know my body will be free,
But my soul will still cry,
"Where will my people be?"

Ebony Lady

Ebony Lady.
Ebony Lady.
You are the light
Of the black man's gold.
You are the life of his heart and soul.

Ebony Lady.
The almighty world has called you a girl,
And your man a boy, but there's something
In your heart that nobody can destroy.
No other woman knows the pain of hate
Better than you.
No other woman can really feel
What you've been through.

Ebony Lady.
If history makes you feel
Out of place because of your race,
Be proud lady, yeah!
Be proud!
Keep a smile on your face!

You're the light of the black man's GOLD.
Life of his heart and soul.

Ebony Lady.
Lady of my blood
And Lady of my love.
Ebony Lady be strong
You deserve a right on.
Be strong.

Love's False Fire

It seems that in one another
We never found true bliss
Because our goals in life have
Never been each others' happiness.

The affairs of your worldly airs
Went straight to your head
So you never really appreciated me
Or the little loving things I did.

True love and desire
Were only a false fire.
For love's magic charm
Had long since gone,
And the fires of desire
Were just a false alarm.

Heartbreak can be hazardous
To your health, when lying to yourself
Because you're in love with somebody
Who's in love with someone else.

It's no good wanting and needing
Somebody until your heart's out of wack
And that very special someone
Still don't want you back.

Because true love and desire
Were only a false fire.
For love's magic charm
Had long since gone,
And the fires of desire
Were just a false alarm.

life ain't about nothin'

life ain't about nothin'
if you can't find
some peace of mind
enough to believe in yo'self
life ain't about nothin'

Scared Straight

For all my soulless sins
And deadly hate, I've been caught up
In the spirit of the Holy Ghost
And scared straight.

As I awake
From my sleep walk through life,
I have forever forsaken the ways
And wiles of the Devil's delight.

The very essence of my life
Has had a change of heart.
My yesterjoys and I have
Become worlds apart.

For all my soulless sins
And deadly hate, I've been caught up
In the spirit of the Holy Ghost
And scared straight.

Through the echoes of troubled times,
The odds 'n' ends of my life
Have survived the beginning of the end.
And even a hell's angel humble from sin
Through faith in God can be born again.

Caught up in the spirit
Of a new way, forever more,
Cuz God has given me so much
To be thankful for.

For all my soulless sins
And deadly hate, I've been caught up
In the spirit of the Holy Ghost
And scared straight.

Keep on Smiling

If you turn a frown upside down,
Then you've turned your whole
World around. Keep on smiling.
Don't let the world get you down.

Keep on smiling to kill the pain.
Let it live no longer, let evil
Grow no stronger.

Keep on smiling
To kill the decay of cancer
Weak minds and hearts portray,
For the world will be a better
Place someday.

Keep on smiling.
Don't let the world get you down.

Pen Man

When I am inspired, there burns a heavenly
Fire in the depth of my heart.
Sometimes, I find that I must set free
All the notions that have given me hope.
To be in love with life is the power of
The poet's scope.
The pen man is enchanted by an electrical
Wonder wave of willpower,
For life has given him a natural task.

POWER
(A Tribute to Minister Louis Farrakhan and the Nation of Islam)

POWER is having the freedom
To be financially free.
POWER is having complete control
Over our economic destiny

POWER is the means by which we
Redirect our economic clout.

POWER is the only color of freedom
Beyond the shadow of a doubt.

POWER is the sum total
Of our sense of self.
POWER is our God-given right
To the Gospel of Wealth.

POWER is the equal opportunity
To be wealthy, wise and free.
POWER is a natural resource
Of Afrikan-American unity.

POWER is the means by which we
Measure life's costly worth.
POWER is people organized
And working for economic rebirth.

Black Family

We are all a part
Of the Master's plan,
Brothers and sisters
In the Family of Man.

I am you,
And you are me.
We are all of
The same life tree.

And whether we
Like it or not,
You and me
Are all we've got

...Black Family.

I Could Never Love Another
(A Tribute to the Temptations)

I truly, truly believe
The Way You Do The Things You Do
I Could Never Love Another
After Loving You.

You're Not An Ordinary Girl
Or An Angel From Above,
But I'm Gonna Keep on Trying
'Till I Win Your Love.

I'm Gonna Make You Love Me
For It's You That I Need,
You're My Everything,
And I Ain't Too Proud To Plead

You're My Little Miss Sweetness
And All I Need From Now On,
'Cause Ain't No Sunshine
Since You've Been Gone.

And I Truly, Truly Believe
The Way You Do The Things You Do
I Could Never Love Another
After Loving You.

Food for Thought

Like the love of money
Is Food for Thought to
The rich and the greedy,
Food stamps are like Life Savers
To the poor and the needy.

A World Without Love

A world without love
Is like a bird without its wings,
It just can't go on anymore.
A world without love can't survive,

It must have love, 'cause God knows
We need love.
A world without love
Is like a man without a heart.
Without love, we have nothing to give,
So how can we live in a world without love,
If we've never really learned to live love.
With all its downfalls, we really haven't
Learned to live at all....
In a world without love.

The Imperial Night

It was a long awaited night
When Ali and Frazier fought that mighty fight.
People came from miles around
To see the end of the big showdown.

There was talk all over the nation
About this great fight sensation.
Ali and Frazier were to meet in the ring
To do their own reputational thing.
Now, the world would finally get to see
The greatest fight that could ever be.
It was just a half past ten, and
I could feel the tension building up within.

As the fighters entered the ring, a voice yelled aloud,
There was a little old man up in the crowd.
He said, "Ali, you are smart and fast that's true,
But Joe Frazier is going to make a fool out of you."

Now, it did not matter that they were of the same race
Because there was so much money involved
that thought was out of place.
As the fight developed and was all on its way,
Ali seemed to get cocky and started to play

It was something to my surprise
To see that Muhammad Ali wasn't so wise.
In the eleventh round, Frazier's left hook staggered Ali
Against the rope.

And from this point on, Ali didn't seem to have much hope.
Then in the fifteenth and final round
Frazier scored the winning knockdown.
Yes, it was truly an Imperial Night
Joe Frazier had won the mighty fight.

But, I still believe that when Ali was in his prime,
He was the greatest fighter of all time.
And even now, if there is ever a return bout,
Ali will not hesitate to knock Frazier out.

First Class Friendship

Let's be the first 'n' forever
To make love a livin' legend.
And through thick 'n' thin we know
That love is our best friend.

In style and class
Let's build a life
For the future on things of the past
With the love we have.

And if our feelings for each other
Never get to be more than a negative win,
Let's be the best of first-class friends
In love's first-class friendship.

We've both reached the bottom of the barrel
In our bag of tricks; we found ourselves
And put away all the silly things we use to
Do for kicks.

There's no heavenly high in livin' a lie
Love is the thing that makes life
Worth livin', and truth is the thing
That makes love worth giving.

And if our feelings for each other
Never get to be more than a negative win,
Let's be the best of first-class friends
In love's first-class friendship.

The Ugly People Poem
(Just Plain Ugly)

This is the ugly people song-poem.
Yes it's true, they have beauty too.
This is the ugly people poem.

If nature didn't give you physical beauty,
Ain't no need ta be blue.
Though you may be ugly as hell,
You're only human too.

Everyone couldn't be beautiful
In every way, so look a little deeper,
And you'll find true bliss in the naked
Beauty of ugliness....

It seems you never smile out loud
In a great big crowd, and while the
World is fast asleep you know that
Beauty cuts deeper than skin deep.

This is the ugly people song-poem.
Yes it's true, they have beauty too.
This is the ugly people poem.

Even the best of beauty
Can go bad; the hard core of happiness can be sad.
And just as coldness be cruel...
A wise man becomes a fool.

This is the ugly people song-poem
Yes it's true, they have beauty too.
This is the ugly people poem.

Black and Blue

The ghetto world has been my life from
A baby. Childhood couldn't help but to
Pass me by; I was conditioned by life
To do or die. When I was a kid,
I never had time to really treasure my

Childhood. But now that I am a man,
Mellow is my mind from experience and
Time, from experience in life itself.

I was just a ghetto kid from the
Rundown side of the world, for I was
Never born to be scholar bound.
But I respected the essence of the
Golden Rule. I played it cool, and
It was a God-send that I made it through
School.

Even now there are forces behind voices
That give me natural hell because
My skin is black. I couldn't ever be
Wrong by standing for my rights and
Coming on strong.

Search for Tomorrow

As the world turns
We stand on the edge
Of night, in search of
Tomorrow's guiding light.

For "In God We Trust" has
Become the true love of life because love is
A many-splintered thing, as we cling to the days
Of our lives in search of the love that nobody
Brings.

For richer, for poorer,
We're all nature's children.
The weak, the meek, and the mild,
The young and the restless,
The old, the peaceful, and the wild.

And with this one life to live,
Through the secret storms of troubled times,
Let us doctor our "sin sick souls"
From the sadness of sorrow as we stand here
On the edge of night
In search of a new tomorrow.

Love Somebody

When livin' a lie for love,
Color life with truth and love's
A natural theme, for you'll find
Peace 'n' pride in the reality of a dream.
Just love somebody.

Sleep walkin' through life,
Your heart smiles a frown.
Soul searchin' lost 'n' found
Fast to sleep on a merry-go-round.

If it's the last thing you do,
Take a hand, to give a hand
To salvation for the family
Of man.

Love somebody!

With this brief, breath of life
In the course of a lifetime,
Learn to love somebody, love somebody
True, and surely somebody will love you.

Just love somebody!

Bleeding Black Hearts

Racism of America the old
Becomes racism of America the young
As bleeding black hearts bleed on.

Tell me how long, how long,
Must our hearts be trampled by the
Powers that be, before we'll know the
Freedom of justice and equality.
America is a dream factory
That produces nightmares of
Ventures untold.
America suffers from the cancer
Of hatefulness that eats the life

Of her body and soul.
And so the conscience of America
Bleeds on internally, without
A smile on the face of her fateful
Future, as bleeding black hearts
Bleed on.

Still A Star In My Heart

I've never tasted
The Big Apple or spent
A day in Hollywood, and I'm
Not sure I would if I could,
But I'm just as much a star
As Hollywood heroes are.
I'm a star in my heart,
Still a star in my heart.
After all's said and done,
I know I'm still a
Special someone.
There's nothing in the world,
The galaxy or the universe
That can make me a fallin' star
Long as I'm a star in my heart.

Let's Talk about It

Before we just split,
walk away and call it quits,
let's sit on down, and talk
about it.

Because if we keep ourselves
in check with love and respect,
while honoring honesty and truth,
the life we live will be love's living proof.

And if we're ready,
willing, and able, let's lay
and play our cards on top
of the table.

Somewhere deep inside,
you hide all your frustrations
and agony, away from me under lock
and key, as though they were a felony.

But we can keep
the dying embers
of our love's light lit,
if we come to an understanding
and simply sit down
And talk about it.

20th Century Fox

Livin' the life
Of the bourgeois,
You were born a brainchild
Of so-called high society.

But as a status seeker
Of nothing less than sweet success,
You forsaked love for hate when you
Were lost 'n found in the cross fires
Of fate.

All your stagnant, stale
And still-born schemes have made you
The faded rose of all your empty-headed
Half-hearted-dreams.

For the unsightly battle scars
Of livin' the life in a fool's paradise
Have made you careless and cold-blooded
To everyone else and left you completely
Headless and just hung up-on yourself.

Walkie-Talkie
Part II

Always tunin' in and turnin' on
Tryin' to catch a line, you're just a
Walkie-Talkie, walkin' 'n' talkin'
All the time.

You can turn a dyin' ember
Into a full-fledged, flame of fire,
And when it comes to somebody else's
Business, you're a real live wire.
Smilin' through the salty-bitter taste of tears
Laughin' 'n' lyin' through all of your fears.

You're the mastermind of the motor mouth
Lip service; you're just a walkin' hot line
Caught up in the grapevine, with live wires
Runnin' through your mind.

Always tunin' in and turnin' on
  Tryin' to catch a line, you're just a
Walkie-Talkie, walkin' 'n' talkin'
  All the time.

Color Me Poetry

Color me the man that cried I am
And that will be my eternal flame.
Color Me Poetry
For nobody knows my name.

I am the living experience.
I am the life-long proof.
Color Me the Poetry
Of nothing but the truth.

I am not to be
Sold nor bought,
So color me a scholar
In the school of thought.
For I Am Poetry!

Color me the native sons
That can't be set apart.
From the poetry of the soul
That's straight from the heart.
Color Me Poetry.

I am the language of love
In the key of life.
I am a way with words
In times of sorrow and strife.
For I Am Poetry!

Let us lift every voice and sing
Of black and unknown bards of long ago.
Color me a song in spite of myself
That all the world might know.
Color Me Poetry.

I am the Middle Passage and after.
You are me and I am you.
We wear the masks of America
Something old, something new.
For I Am Poetry!

Color me low to high
And high to low.
I am the dark symphony
Of the unsung hero.

Yet I too sing America.
Color me Othello, the Moor
I am the souls of black folk,
The spook who sat by the door.
Color Me Poetry.

Color me a love child
Lost in the Promise Land.
I am a poem for black hearts
Going to meet the man.

Color me a "B" movie
That holds all eyes.

That will not be televised.
Color Me Poetry.

Color me the undercurrent
In America's mainstream.
I am like the ripple on a pond
In the all American dream.

I am fantasy,
Fiction and fact
Color me the shadow
And well the act.
For I Am Poetry!

Color me the rose
And the thorn.
I am the timeless hopes
Of dreams yet unborn.

I am for my people
A portrait of Pride.
Color me the Negro who speaks
Of rivers deep down inside.
For I Am Poetry!

White Supremacy
(A Tribute to Dr. Frances Cress Welsing & Mr. Neely Fuller)

As long as white supremacy
Is alive and well
A white man's heaven
Is a black man's hell.

Uncle Sam and Jim Crow
Are the archdeceivers of the game
And that old skinhead, Ku Klux spirit
Is still the same.

As a manchild of the sun
I've got melanin on my mind
Can't afford to be simply
Deaf, Dumb and Blind
When white supremacy
Is the bottom line.

And as long as white supremacy
Is alive and still kickin' ass
Freedom, Justice and Equality
Will never come to pass.

Many look, but only
Few ever really see
The most unjust dynamic
In the world is white supremacy.

The Cress theory of color
Conscious confrontation
Is about the fear of white
Genetic annihiliation.

Too white to be black, Too black
To be white in this man's land
For the way of the white minded
Negro is apart of the master plan.

The Chess Board of white supremacy
Will pull the game of real life over our eyes
'Cause the wishy-washy ways of white folk
Are the ways of the wickly-wise.

But when we know the sum
Total of our sense of self
We sure can't afford
To be nobody else.

And as long as white supremacy
Is alive and well
A white man's heaven
Is a black man's hell.

For Many look, but only
Few ever really see
The most unjust dynamic
In the world is white supremacy.

Quin-Essence
(A Tribute to Quincy Jones)

You're somethin' some kinda special
You're always right on 'Q'
The secret garden of your love for music
Will always be a part of you.

With just a taste of your
Ever-ready Razzamatazz
You can swing into some bluenote
Easy listenin' kool-jazz.

Or you can get all rapped up
In some back in the day be-bop
Then fall into the funk of some
Soul rockin' doo-whop
And top it all off with
A dash of today's hip hop.

When it comes to a mindful message
In the music, you're the dude
A master maestro of mellow madness
With a pleasantly pleasing attitude.

You put it all back on the block
'Cause everything's on the kue
And the way you make me feel
I just can't stop lovin' you.

Your rhapsody in harmony
Turns on the action, all the way strong
And without your golden touch
What good is a song.

Without your thunder thumbs
And lightin' licks, of love by name
The mind set of music today
Really, just ain't the same.

But when you know, you got what
It takes 'cause that's where it's at
"What makes you feel like
Doin' stuff like that?"

By: Daniel R. Queen
Copyright 1990
All Rights Reserved

"THE GODFATHER OF SOUL"
(A Tribute to James Brown)

I feel good, I'm sayin' it loud
I'm proud to be black
So get up offa that thang
It's time for the pay back.

Bewildered, Livin' in America
You've earned your just due
You got the super-soul power
And all know it's true.

When doin' it to death, make it funky
And the Godfather's on the goodfoot for sure
I feel alright, so let yourself go
And just give me some more
It's too funky in here, but I don't mind
Give it up or turn it loose
We're gonna have a funky good time.

There was a time, good god, I'd pop corn
To the mashed potatoes, till I was soak 'n' wet
Slide into the James Brown, and break out
In a cold sweat.

Hit me, I got the feelin'
Gonna put it to the test
It's a brand new day, but
Bro: Brown don't take no mess.

There it is, I'm a greedy man
Beyond all conscious control
But try me, I'm Mr. Dynamite
The Godfather of pure soul.

By: Daniel R. Queen
Copyright 1990
All Rights Reserved

"THE MOST DIVINE ONE"
(A Tribute to Sarah Vaughan)

You're the once in a lifetime
Quintessential Queen Divine
The finest voice in all of Jazz
The one and only, one of a kind.

You had a smooth, but rich pitch
In a sultry, sassy tone
You were a livin' legend that gave
Of yourself in a style of your own.

With a great gift of song
That was second to none
Heaven knows, you were
Truly the most Divine One.

You never sang the same song
The same way twice
The way you worked wonders
With words, was pure paradise.

You were the missin' angel
From the divine choir
An elegant earth angel
Here to create and inspire
The makin' of a master miracle
With a voice of heavenly fire.

Your mainstay in music
Was your mastery of self control
The divine sassy Ms. Sarah
Had a tantalizin' touch of pure black gold.

And from here to eternity
Your just due can never be overdone
Your uncanny ability, was most unique
For you were the one and only Divine One.

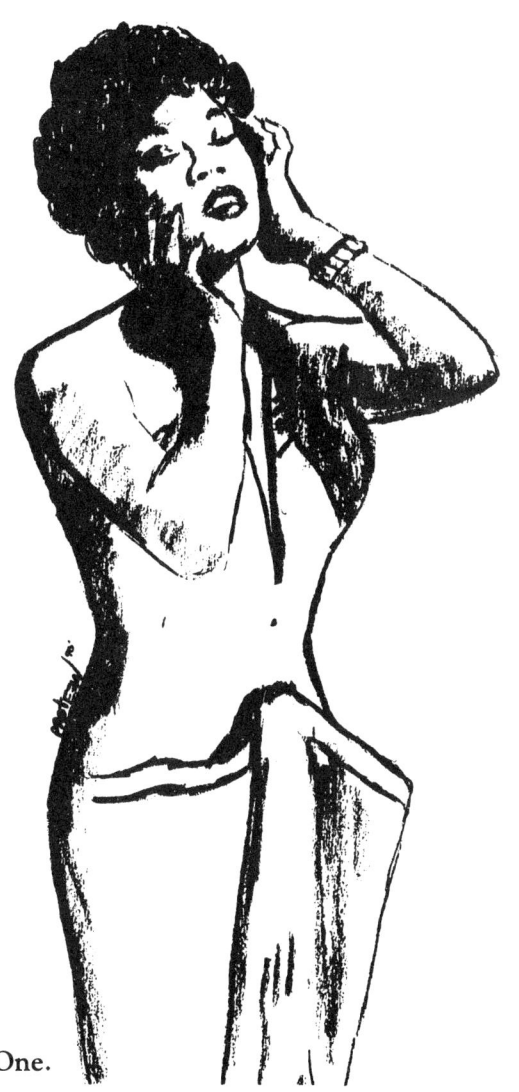

By: Daniel R. Queen
Copyright 1990
All Rights Reserved

CONSCIOUS CONTROL
(A Tribute to Dr. Carter G. Woodson)

Trapped and trained to think
With somebody else's mind
Caught up in the method of the maddness
By a master design.

MA's, JD's, and MS's
An MBA, and a Ph.D
Without the knowledge of self
Don't mean a thing to me
It's all ignorant academics at its best
Like the educated fool, full of B.S.

Highly miseducated misfits
Will keep you chained and bound
Every time you try to get up
They'll pull you back down.

Symptoms of this sickness
Of the soul
Is simply miseducation
By Conscious Control.

By: Daniel R. Queen
Copyright 1990
All Rights Reserved